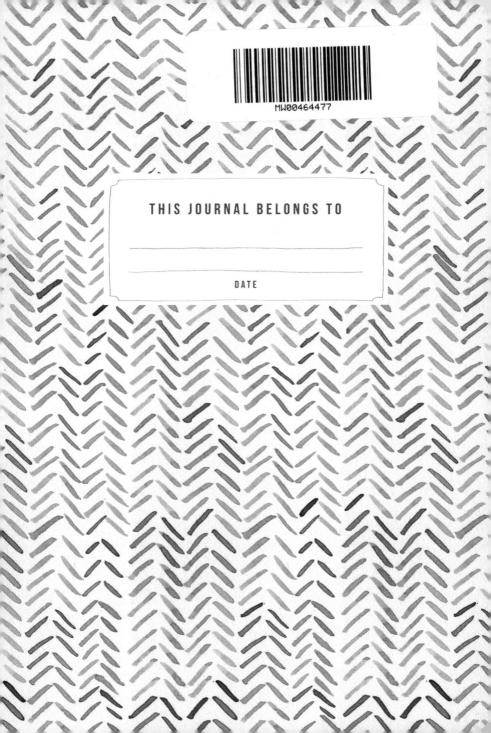

THIS JOURNAL BELONGS TO

_____

DATE

LIVING

freely

AND

lightly

EMILY LEX

HARVEST HOUSE PUBLISHERS
EUGENE, OREGON

Published in association with Jenni Burke of Illuminate Literary Agency: www.illuminateliterary.com

Cover and interior design by Leah Beachy

Living Freely and Lightly

Text and artwork copyright © 2022 by Emily Lex
Published by Harvest House Publishers
Eugene, Oregon 97408
www.harvesthousepublishers.com

ISBN 978-0-7369-8041-8 (pbk.)

Printed in China

22 23 24 25 26 27 28 29 30 /RDS—LB / 10 9 8 7 6 5 4 3 2 1

CONTENTS

• • • • •

A Note from Emily | 4

PART ONE | 13
An Invitation to Recover Your Life

PART TWO | 49
An Invitation to Take a Real Rest

PART THREE | 87
An Invitation to Learn the Unforced Rhythms of Grace

PART FOUR | 123
An Invitation to Live Freely and Lightly

For Your Journey | 160

A NOTE FROM EMILY

It's funny how certain phrases and names can stick so firmly, isn't it? I can barely remember what we did last weekend, but I will never forget the words of my sixth-grade teacher: "Emily, lighten up." My face blushed red, and I turned so no one would see my tears. I was embarrassed and felt scolded and ashamed that I had disappointed my favorite teacher with my overly serious, overly perfectionist, overly concerned-with-what-others-think-of-me ways.

Lighten up.

I don't think he meant anything mean; he was completely accurate in identifying my need to chill out. But it hurt because it collided head-on with what I was leaning on to prove that I was enough. Here's the thing: When you feel like your value is based on what you do and how well you do it, *everything* becomes really important, and you will do all you can to make sure everything is done just how you think it ought to be done or how you think it's expected to be done. Your identity is at stake!

But what if this isn't actually true? (Hint: It isn't true!). Instead of informing the questions of our value with our behaviors and outward actions or listening only to what our society or family or we say about ourselves, what if we believed what God says about us? What if we take my teacher's advice and *lighten up?*

The weight of pleasing others is too heavy. The burden of

trying to prove yourself worthy is too much. It's tiring to hustle for significance, exhausting to be bossed around by insecurity, and no matter how hard you try, eventually self-effort will fail to satisfy. I know that's not very good news, but this is: Jesus says, "Come to me, all you who are weary and burdened, and I will give you rest" (Matthew 11:28). Or, in other words, "My child, lighten up."

Because of Jesus, you can remove from your shoulders the weight of other people's approval and instead tune your ears and focus your eyes on what God says about you and how he would have you live. Can you imagine moving through your day with the confidence of knowing that who you are in Christ is enough and never too much? Knowing deep down that you are okay not because of anything you do or do not do but because a good, kind, merciful God looks at you with tenderness through the sacrifice of Jesus on your behalf ? What a gift!

In my first book, an illustrated memoir called *Freely and Lightly,* I share the story of how God invites us to move from a place of anxiety, insecurity and self-reliance to peace, rest, and hope as we trust in him. Over the course of a handful of years, this miracle of transformation took place in my heart, and while it required letting go of what I thought I needed, I discovered that Jesus has a much better way for us to live. His invitation to live abundantly with him—not just in eternity, but *here* and *now*—changes lives. It absolutely changed mine.

This journal is a tool you can use to move toward this new, restful way of living. Whether you journey through this while reading *Freely and Lightly* or as its own thing, I pray it will meet you right where you're at. It combines thought-provoking questions with space for self-reflection, Scriptures you can ponder, art to encourage you, and creative practices to help you notice and name what the Holy Spirit is revealing to you on your spiritual transformation journey. Every question, Bible verse, prompt, and exercise has been instrumental in helping me learn more about living freely and lightly, and I hope they will be beneficial to you as well.

Like the book *Freely and Lightly*, the journal is divided into four invitations:

- *Part one:* Jesus invites you to **recover your life** as you recognize your need for a new way of living.

- *Part two:* He invites you to take a **real rest** as you open your hands to surrender the things that are keeping you bound.

- *Part three:* You are invited to **learn his unforced rhythms of grace** as you get to know his true character, and in turn, your own.

- *Part four:* He invites you to **live freely and lightly**, finding deep peace and satisfaction as you offer your gifts to the world in your own unique way.

We'll begin and end each part with a simple prayer. You are welcome (encouraged!) to use the accompanying journal pages to express any hopes, fears, questions, and desires that come to mind. I have found journaling my prayers to be one of the best ways to process my own feelings and hear what the Holy Spirit has to say to me. I hope this will be an encouraging practice for you too.

You'll also find a few handpicked Bible verses to remind you of the promises, declarations, and character of God. One way you might use these spaces is to look up the verse in a different translation. Sometimes a rephrasing will spark imagination, insight, or connection in a fresh way. Write down any phrases, words, or meanings that speak to you, and spend time being curious about how the Lord wants to encourage you through his Word.

I know talking about these practices is so much easier than doing them because our lives are so full, but give yourself the gift of time with this journal. Something truly powerful happens when we slow down, get quiet, and make space in our hectic heads to get alone with God.

One more reminder: Before you begin a prayer, prompt, or practice, don't forget to take a breath and acknowledge the presence of the Holy Spirit. He is with you and in you, and nothing can be accomplished without his wise and gracious counsel.

I am so pleased to be the friend to link arms with you as you turn each page. I pray this journal will be a delightful place to take a breath—a deep and sacred place to hear the Holy Spirit whisper his love to you and a practical tool for exploration into the abundant life Jesus has for you.

Xo,

Are you tired?
Worn out? Burned out on religion?
Come to me.
Get away with me and you'll
recover your life.
I'll show you how to take
a real rest.

Walk with me and work with me —
watch how I do it.
Learn the unforced rhythms of grace.
I won't lay anything heavy
or ill-fitting on you.
Keep company with me and you'll learn
to live freely and lightly.

MATTHEW 11:28-30 MSG

As you begin this journal, what is the hope you have for yourself?

What do you most need to hear God say to you,

about you,

and about himself?

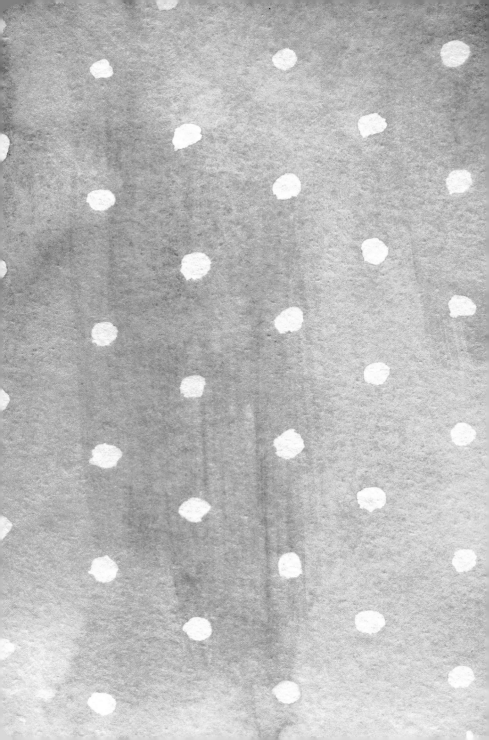

PART ONE

AN INVITATION TO
RECOVER YOUR LIFE

INTRODUCTION

Sometimes God gets our attention with a loud crash of circumstances, shaking us awake to the need for a new way of living. But I wonder if more often it's a gentle, subtle, slow waking up. Insecurities popping up here, questions coming to the surface there, small things that point to bigger things that tell us perhaps what we've been saying is fine is not actually fine at all.

Jesus offers a vision for the good, abundant life, but if you're like me, you've been settling for a counterfeit for a very long time. The thing is, it's easy to fall back to sleep. To be lulled into thinking the dissatisfaction inside you is made up, the questions about your true identity are unimportant and too big, the unbecoming behavior just needs to be modified with discipline and determination.

But instead, what if these are signposts pointing you in the right direction—toward health, healing, and wholeness? If that's the case, then let's wake up and take notice of those important signs!

Your life can be made new again, restored to its original purpose, full of peace and hope. The first step to making a change of any kind is to become aware of the need for change, so this is where we'll begin. With the help of the Holy Spirit, use this section to engage in the spiritual work of honest exploration, listening, reflecting, truth telling, and peering under the surface of your behavior to discover any places where you're tangled up and kept from the abundant life Jesus is offering.

As you recognize where you may have veered off course, please be gentle with yourself and remember that God is so full of grace. This journey is about learning, remembering, and clinging to the truth that will set you free. Will it be a little uncomfortable? For sure. But it is absolutely worth it.

This is an invitation to recover your life.

Lord Jesus, you know my heart, you know my fears, you know my story, and still you look at me with such love, ready to embrace me when I come. Here I am. Help me be brave as I peer deeply, take account, and admit my need for your healing as you remake me into who you always intended me to be. Will you open my eyes and heart to the ways I am trusting in places that are not worthy to be trusted and looking for satisfaction where it will not be found? Will you, in your most tender kindness, show me where my life needs to change? Wake me up, Lord, to the truth that YOU are better than anything else on earth. I come to you tired and weary; please be gentle with me.

Share your heart with God.

_____

_____

_____

_____

_____

_____

_____

_____

_____

_____

_____

_____

_____

_____

_____

_____

_____

_____

_____

Amen ♥

recover (v.):

To get back again: regain. To regain normal health, poise, or status.

Jesus invites you to come to him to recover your life.

When have you had a sense of God's love and acceptance that gave you a glimpse of your authentic self?

What areas can you identify that need recovering?

"Are you tired? Do you feel a deep unsettledness within? When you look at your life—honestly look and *see*—are you trying to fill or numb a hint of dissatisfaction with your own striving and proving, and it's just not working? Is the question *Who am I?* or *What is my purpose?* or *Am I enough?* on the tip of your tongue, but you're too afraid to speak it into existence? Oh, friend, you are not alone. These questions and feelings, while uncomfortable and disorienting, are so good. Don't push them away! This is God waking you up to abundant life. This is him gently shaking you from the dull slumber of 'fine' so you can step across the line into wholehearted freedom. The bravest thing you can do is open up your hands and turn your feet toward the path that leads to new, flourishing growth as you accept Jesus's call to live freely and lightly. It's truly the most beautiful of all invitations."

Freely and Lightly, page 21

How is God waking you? What do you notice happening that may be a sign that God is trying to get your attention?

What questions are you most needing answered?

Jesus says, "Come to me, all you who are weary and burdened, and I will give you rest" (Matthew 11:28).

What burdens do you carry?

List the things that add to your weariness. Place internal factors (such as a specific insecurity, worry, or fear) inside the circle, and put external factors (like your schedule, a deadline, or a newborn baby) outside the circle.

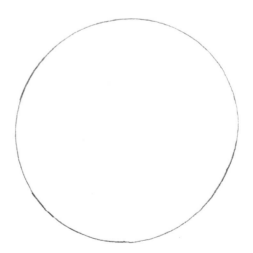

Now imagine handing over to God what weighs heavily on you. Is there an image that comes to mind? Draw it here to represent how you feel as you envision God taking your burdens from you.

Do not be anxious
about anything
but in every situation,
by prayer and petition,
with Thanksgiving
present your requests
to God.

PHILIPPIANS 4:6

Look up this verse in another Bible translation and rewrite it here.
What stands out to you?

THE FOUR PATHS

The parable of the sower in Matthew 13:1-23 describes four paths.
Look up and read that passage. *Then, using the sketch below, draw
in details as given in the story.*

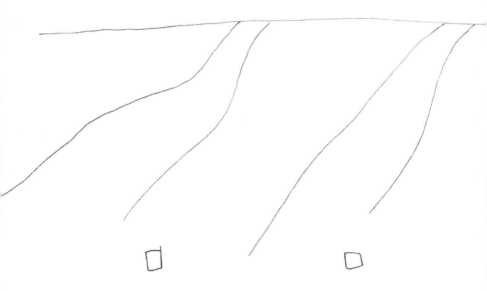

PATH ONE:
I have heard the good news,
but it doesn't make sense,
so I have dismissed it.

PATH TWO:
I heard and accepted, but
with life's difficulties,
I have let it go.

Think about the plants, textures, stones, weeds, and views you might find along each path, and add words to indicate what those represent in your life.

Check the box of the path of faith in Jesus you most identify with There's no wrong answer! Be honest.

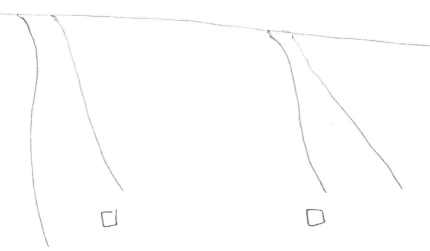

PATH THREE:
I accepted Jesus as my Savior but am distracted by life's many temptations. I'm dancing between faith and doubt.

PATH FOUR:
I have fully embraced that God is in charge of my life, and I trust that blessings come from obeying and living according to his countercultural ways.

You can be saved without being free. Eternally secure (praise Jesus) but living insecure, unsettled, and fearful now.

How does this realization shine a light on how you are feeling or doing life right now?

I'm fine (I'm not fine)

A friend pulled me aside on a particularly emotional day and helped me realize I was stubbornly grasping onto "fine" in most areas of life. I was fine. My marriage was fine. My relationships were fine. My health was fine. She asked a question that changed the course of my life, and I'll ask it to you as well: What if there is better? Not better in the sense of more or boast-worthy, but redeemed, healed, restored, recovered to its original design. What if releasing the things you label as "fine," digging into your insecurities, and asking questions could uncover a life so much better than fine?

In the space below, list the areas of your life you would call fine.

FINE

Describe how each "fine" area would look or feel if it became better. Ask God to work his powerful healing over each item on your list.

BETTER

"It's okay to admit you are not fine. In fact, it's the first step to freedom." *Freely and Lightly,* page 58

Think of a time when you have felt deep contentment.

Why do you think that moment, activity, or season of life nurtured a sense of satisfaction?

Where do you currently feel dissatisfied and discontent?

What are you reaching for to fill this? (Consider material possessions, achievements, relationships, and patterns of behavior.)

For he satisfies
the longing soul,
and the hungry soul
he fills with
good things.

PSALM 107:9 ESV

WHO AM I?

Check the boxes of the questions that resonate most deeply within you. Add any additional questions that come to the surface as you uncover what your soul is most longing to know.

- ☐ Am I loved?
- ☐ Am I good?
- ☐ Am I valued?
- ☐ Am I special?
- ☐ Am I competent?
- ☐ Am I safe?
- ☐ Am I provided for?
- ☐ Am I respected?
- ☐ Am I significant?

- ☐ Am I enough?
- ☐ Am I too much?
- ☐ Am I forgotten?
- ☐ Am I needed?
- ☐ Am I wanted?
- ☐ _____
- ☐ _____
- ☐ _____
- ☐ _____

I sat alone on the beach, knees tucked up, facing the vast Pacific Ocean when the question finally came tumbling out of my heart: *Who am I?* I felt lost. I knew the core of me was in there somewhere, but I couldn't find my way out with all the titles, stories, labels, and masks I was buried under. These were the things I was clinging to with the hope of answering the question under the question ... but they actually led to a lost sense of true identity.

Is there a time in your life when you have felt this same sense of lostness? What were the circumstances that led you there?

Use this space to add words, images, and doodles to note the feelings, questions, and answers to your Who am I? moment.

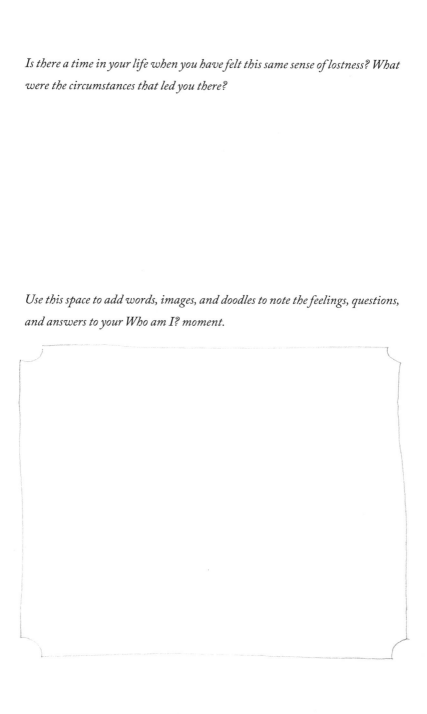

This Is Me

I LIKE THIS ABOUT ME

Traits, gifts, and strengths that make me who I am.

ROOM FOR IMPROVEMENT

Labels, images, and masks that don't belong in my recovered life.

And we all,
who with unveiled faces
contemplate the Lord's glory,
are being transformed
into his image
with ever-increasing glory,
which comes from the Lord,
who is the Spirit

2 CORINTHIANS 3:18

How does this verse refresh your sense of identity?

Signposts

The Holy Spirit loves to speak to his children. Sometimes it's hard to notice, with all the noise of daily life swirling around, but when we do, it's such a good idea to pay attention!

Use this space to mark moments, song lyrics, Scriptures, podcasts, conversations, and other gifts that have pointed you to Jesus to claim your true identity.

EVERYDAY BEAUTY

Just as the Spirit of God whispered to me, he says the same to you ... "I see you. I have not forgotten you. And I'm right here with you now. You might not know who you are anymore, but I do. It's time to heal, to tell the truth, to stop trying to fill yourself with things that weren't made to satisfy. You are worshipping the wrong things. Come to me, you who are weary and heavily burdened, and I will give you rest."

Freely and Lightly, page 67

• • • • •

Imagine yourself being swept up in God's embrace and hearing only loving words, not reprimands, spoken over you. *What is God telling you about yourself that you have longed to hear?*

Come to me

Rewrite these agreements as a way of accepting Jesus's invitation to come to him. Include additional statements as the Holy Spirit guides you.

I want purpose. I will come to you to find it.
I want a secure identity. I will come to you to find it.
I want to feel significance. I will come to you to find it.
I want belonging. I will come to you to find it.
I want peace. I will come to you to find it.

Jesus, you wrap your arms around me, so much less concerned about my bad behavior than you are about my precious heart. I am so grateful. I linger here because I need to know I am loved. I need to know I'm not forgotten. I need to know who I am.

Please recover my life.

Amen ✓

PART TWO

AN INVITATION TO TAKE A
REAL REST

INTRODUCTION

You know that feeling at the end of the day when you finally take out the ponytail you've been wearing for hours? There's a dull ache and it doesn't feel all that great, but you know it won't linger for long. You rub your head where the rubber band once was, massaging away the tenderness, and snuggle into your pillow. Ahhh … it's time to rest!

The thing about rest of all kinds, from the quick midafternoon nap to the soul-deep variety that we're after here, is that it requires an undoing, a releasing, surrender. You trade in something (time, productivity, a nice hairdo), trusting that what you'll receive in the end will be so much better than what you gave up.

Often the things that are tangling you up and keeping you from real rest are the very things you're clinging to. They are the beliefs and patterns of behavior you lean into, thinking they are what you need to be safe, provided for, significant, and successful. This is a paradox—when we let go of these unfruitful efforts to prove ourselves worthy, we make room for God to prove himself worthy and in turn, set our souls at ease.

The rest Jesus invites you to experience is not a one-time act, like taking a nap or a vacation or a mid-workout water break. Rather, it's the calm inner disposition of a secure identity that no longer feels the need to self-protect and self-promote. Jesus opens his arms and makes this curious exchange: your anxious thoughts for his perfect peace.

This is an invitation to take a real rest.

God, I long for a deep inner disposition of rest. If that requires surrender, then here I am, ready to let go. Will you shine a light on the places that need adjusting in my heart and actions? Help me see where and why I turn to the things of the world to satisfy longings that only you can fill. Please give me the patience, insight, and determination to release, to trust, and to let you chisel away the hurts, fears, and trappings that are keeping me from true, abundant life.

My hands are open.

Share your heart with God.

_____

_____

_____

_____

_____

_____

_____

_____

_____

_____

_____

_____

_____

_____

_____

_____

_____

_____

_____

Amen ♥

rest (n.):

peace of mind or spirit

Jesus invites you to take a real rest.

When have you experienced peace of mind or spirit?

What does rest look like to you? What are your favorite restful activities?

When it comes to your heart, mind, and soul, in what areas can you see your need for rest?

"As we accept Jesus's invitation to find real rest, we have to start with surrender. When we release our tight grip on our lives, we allow old patterns and wrong ways of thinking to fall away.... This letting go makes way for new, beautiful, abundant growth....

"The rest Jesus offers is *true* rest for our souls that we can find only when we let go of unfruitful efforts to prove ourselves worthy and make room for God to bring forth new life. We participate in this growth by letting go of our mistaken beliefs about where identity, purpose, and belonging are found and allow him to restore our hearts to the truth."

Freely and Lightly, pages 79–80

What behaviors or beliefs do you hold on to tightly that you may need to release?

Consider the following options and mark any that resonate with you. Write in other behaviors or temptations that come to mind.

- ☐ control
- ☐ comparison
- ☐ busyness
- ☐ comfort

- ☐ self-reliance
- ☐ _____
- ☐ _____
- ☐ _____

Write down observations, thoughts, or questions as you reflect on what keeps you from real rest.

He cuts off every branch in me
that bears no fruit,
while every branch that does
bear fruit he prunes
so that it will be
even more fruitful

JOHN 15:2

ON DISPLAY
IN NATURE

Spend some time outdoors. Take a walk, sit on the porch, or spread a blanket under a tree. As you look around, where do you see an example of surrender? Where do you witness something released turned into something new? Draw what you discover and consider how God might use this example to build trust with you.

Control

The desire for control has a sneaky way of showing up daily, tripping up even the most unsuspecting. It's in our nature to want power, to think our way is the best way, and to put our own desires ahead of any other. This tendency toward control can show up in big ways but might be most evident in the little preferences and particularities that pop up during the day. Here's a great way to figure out whether control is a trouble spot for you: Pay attention to the impact of your preferences. Do others feel loved by you, or scolded, dismissed, and criticized?

• ◆ •

Fill in the blanks to help identify if (and where) control is showing up in your life:

I am particular about _____

because _____ .

When it doesn't go how I want, I _____ ,

and the impact is _____ .

I am particular about _____
because _____.

When it doesn't go how I want, I _____,
and the impact is _____.

I am particular about _____
because _____.

When it doesn't go how I want, I _____,
and the impact is _____.

I am particular about _____
because _____.

When it doesn't go how I want, I _____,
and the impact is _____.

Control isn't all bad. The desire for excellence and order is a beautiful gift from God that we can use for his glory. *How has control served you and those around you well?*

But control can certainly leap over the line into an unhealthy place. *How is it hindering your sense of rest and peace?*

When you reflect on the role of control in your life, what do you think it protects you from? If it was taken from you, what are you afraid could happen?

Describe your emotions and the outcome when you have surrendered control of a moment, situation, or relationship to God.

When the desire to be changed by real rest surpasses the desire to be right and in charge, something loosens and prepares you to be still and know God. *Use this space to talk to him about letting go of the need for control.*

_____

_____

_____

_____

_____

_____

_____

_____

_____

_____

_____

_____

_____

_____

Amen ✓

Comparison

They say comparison is the thief of joy, and I *mostly* agree. Where I think this statement falls short is that it blames the wrong thing. It's not so much that comparison is the problem; instead, the true enemy is the self-obsession that causes us to make judgments about our value based on self-imposed standards of measuring up. I often do this in a split-second with little forethought, and it makes every single thing about *me*. Which is precisely the problem. It shows just how utterly insecure and utterly prideful we are at the same time, which robs us of joyfully celebrating the successes of others, finding contentment in our own lives, and experiencing the quiet confidence Jesus offers us when we rest in his opinion of us.

Think of a time when you were stuck in the grip of comparison. What was it about? Who were you comparing yourself to?

Dig down a little deeper ... what were you really looking to answer? Is there an insecurity you want proven false? Is there a worry you are looking to validate?

CAPTURE YOUR COMPARISON THOUGHTS

Pay attention to the comparisons that run through your mind. On the left thought bubble, write down the comparison narratives that most often play in your mind. In the bubble on the right, rewrite the statement as an affirmation that your value is not determined by how you measure up.

If you gave yourself a break from looking around to see who is watching and approving of you, and instead turned your eyes toward Jesus, what might that do to your perspective, confidence, and level of anxiety?

let us run
with endurance
the race that lies
before us
Keeping our eyes on Jesus
the source and perfecter
of our faith.

HEBREWS 12:1-2 HCSB

busyness

Don't get me wrong—I like having fun things on the calendar to look forward to. I like a checklist and feeling productive, and I know so many wonderful people who much prefer being active to sitting silently for hours on end. There is no one perfect way to move through our lives, so please feel zero shame if you are the type who thrives when there are things to do.

However, it is possible to lean in heavily to good things in life to avoid what's really happening underneath. The gift of presence—with the people around you, yourself, and God—allows for deeper relationships, more contentment, and a slower, more peaceful and aware existence. It sounds wonderful, doesn't it? So, what keeps you so mightily distracted all the time? Let's see if we can uncover some of the insecurities hidden behind a busy life.

Do silence and an open schedule make you anxious? Sad? Excited?

What are the go-to distractions and activities you use to avoid fully engaging with people around you? With yourself?

BUSYNESS INVENTORY

Fill in the chart to see where you can eliminate excess.

TASK	HAVE TO DO	WANT TO DO	LET IT GO
_____	☐	☐	☐
_____	☐	☐	☐
_____	☐	☐	☐
_____	☐	☐	☐
_____	☐	☐	☐
_____	☐	☐	☐
_____	☐	☐	☐
_____	☐	☐	☐
_____	☐	☐	☐
_____	☐	☐	☐
_____	☐	☐	☐
_____	☐	☐	☐
_____	☐	☐	☐
_____	☐	☐	☐
_____	☐	☐	☐
_____	☐	☐	☐
_____	☐	☐	☐

Think about what triggers you to seek out a distraction. Is there a common time of day? Emotion? Circumstance? Consider how the distraction is serving you in some way. Write to explore whether there is a more restful option or mindful way to serve that same need.

Comfort

At first glance, choosing to stay comfortable seems to be about the wonderfulness of all things comfortable. Who doesn't love a cozy pair of slippers and the familiarity of a regular routine? But what if that's not actually what clinging to our comfort zones is all about? With the help of the Holy Spirit, let's look at what you consider safe and comfortable to help shed light on what things you are afraid of. After all, this is likely what you are avoiding by creating the protective walls of a comfort zone. As you step beyond what is comfortable, may you find growth, freedom, and true rest.

Share a story about a time when your desire to build up a boundary ended up shining a light on a deep truth about you.

Using the circle, define your comfort zone through words and pictures. *What is inside? What is outside?*

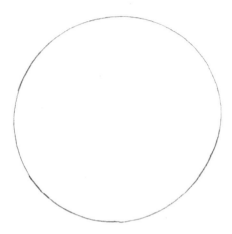

What do your comforts say about what you are afraid of? What are they helping you avoid?

How do those fears play out in your perception of yourself? Of God?

self-reliance

Am I the only one who struggles with trust? I have no problem with trust during the minor, mostly inconsequential things, but when it comes to full, complete, lay down my life, let someone else be in charge, don't depend on myself type of trust, that's hard. Trust requires submission and the belief that the one you're putting your trust in has your best interest in mind.

On one hand, self-reliance is a desirable quality. It means you are a responsible human and can take care of yourself. On the other hand, it can undermine the beauty and vulnerability that is displayed through leaning on others—and ultimately, God.

How do you see the tension between trust and self-reliance playing out in your life?

Let's take a self-reliance inventory.

THINGS I WANT TO DO MYSELF   WHY?

☐
☐
☐
☐
☐
☐
☐
☐

THINGS I NEED GOD'S HELP WITH   WHY?

☐
☐
☐
☐
☐
☐
☐
☐

When has self-reliance been helpful to you?

When has it hindered growth, trust, or a closer relationship?

In what ways are you trusting in your own ability instead of trusting that Jesus has the best way to live? Write an honest note to God expressing your feelings about trust and self-reliance.

TAKE THOUGHTS CAPTIVE

The path to abundant life comes into view when we bring our insecurities into the light and put them to rest.

As you uncover the insecurities (lies) you believe about yourself, list them here.

insecurity

□
□
□
□
□
□
□
□
□
□
□
□
□
□
□
□

Therefore, if anyone is in Christ, he is a new creation. The old has passed away; behold, the new has come.
2 Corinthians 5:17 ESV

Now bring those insecurities into the light and ask God to show you what's true. Look for past experiences, Scriptures, and promises to combat the lies with truth.

truth

- [ ]
- [ ]
- [ ]
- [ ]
- [ ]
- [ ]
- [ ]
- [ ]
- [ ]
- [ ]
- [ ]
- [ ]
- [ ]
- [ ]
- [ ]
- [ ]

Lord, I come before you more aware of how I turn to the things of this world for identity, and I acknowledge the ways this keeps me trapped in a life that is not truly alive and free. You have so much more for me. Thank you for being a God who listens, who is in control, and who is faithful to do all you have promised. Help me notice what I add to my life as a distraction from being still or from tending to my heart needs. Show me the wonders of rest for my mind, body, and spirit so that I hunger for it more than I thirst for busyness.

I'm so grateful to lean into your strength today.

Amen ♦

PART THREE

AN INVITATION TO LEARN THE
UNFORCED RHYTHMS OF GRACE

INTRODUCTION

Will you do something with me? Hold your arms outstretched in front of you with your hands firmly fisted, thumbs pointing down. Now turn your hands over and open them up. I remember standing on my front porch doing this one summer morning when I needed a physical reminder of the spiritual work that was happening inside. It is a helpful way to visualize the transformation taking place in you. Take a moment to acknowledge the growth. You've moved from tightly grasping the things you thought would bring you satisfaction to a place of surrender, with hands wide open.

So, what now? Well, if you've ever cleaned out a junk drawer, you know how this next part goes. Once you pull everything out— the stacks of half-used sticky notes, piles of pens, scissors, broken pencils, crinkled receipts, stray rubber bands, and batteries that you're not sure are new or used—you keep what you need and toss the rest.

You could push in the cleaned-out drawer and move along, but you know it's only a matter of time before it junks itself right back up. Instead, you must find a new method of organization, perhaps with dividers or containers or labels. So you adopt a better way of using the junk drawer to make it less junky. The same is true of your heart, mind, and soul.

Now is the beautiful part (my personal favorite!), where new thoughts, beliefs, and ways of living refill those open hands. Jesus has set a cadence and invites you to follow his example to live a restful, purposeful, peace-filled life. And as you do, something incredible happens: Your vision of who you are, who God is, and what a truly satisfying life looks like begins to line up with Jesus's vision of these same things.

This is an invitation to learn the unforced rhythms of grace.

Jesus, you have invited me to learn your unforced rhythms of grace, to watch how you do life and model my own after you. I long for soul-deep rest, for a secure identity that does not change based on how others feel about me or how I feel about myself, but only by what you say of me. You promise that your yoke is easy and your burden is light. Help me to see your goodness, to trust you completely, and to fall in step with you.

Share your heart with God.

_____
_____
_____
_____
_____
_____
_____
_____
_____
_____
_____
_____
_____
_____
_____
_____
_____
_____
_____
_____
_____
_____
_____

Amen ♥

rhythm (v.):

A strong, regular, repeated pattern of
movement or sound.

Jesus invites you to learn the unforced rhythms of grace.

What comes to mind when you hear the phrase "unforced rhythms of grace"?

How have you experienced walking in step with Jesus?

Which life areas do you identify as needing to align with how Jesus encourages you to live?

"Jesus has a solution for all of us who wish to live in an easier, lighter, more meaningful, and purposeful way: 'Walk with me and work with me,' he says. 'Watch how I do it. Learn the unforced rhythms of grace. I won't lay anything heavy or ill-fitting on you' (Matthew 11:28-30 MSG).

"In more traditional versions of the Bible, this is the part that references a yoke, as in 'take my yoke upon you and learn from me' (Matthew 11:29). A yoke is a wooden beam placed over the shoulders of two animals (like oxen or donkeys) to connect them so they can move in unison as they pull a plow or a cart. At first glance, the metaphor seems odd. *We're talking about rest, Jesus. Why the mention of a tool used for hard, laborious work?* But scooch in a little closer and you'll see what he's getting at: Life requires effort. Jesus never promises a trouble-free, easy-peasy existence. There is beauty and goodness and truth, of course, but also difficulty, sadness, loss, and hardship. We are not made to hide, be numb, and sleepwalk all our days; we are made to be alive, and life requires effort."

Freely and Lightly, pages 151–153

When you think of working and walking with Jesus, is there a picture or image that comes to mind? Draw it here.

SPIRITUAL DISCIPLINES

SOLITUDE

Get alone (either physically or in your mind) with God.

SILENCE

Turn off all man-made noise (a quiet walk in the woods is still considered silence).

PRAYER

Have a conversation with God.

FASTING

Deny yourself physically to experience spiritual sustenance.

CONFESSION

Bring secrets into the light.

FELLOWSHIP

Engage in face-to-face relationships.

What spiritual disciplines do you currently practice? How has this encouraged your faith?

Spiritual disciplines are practices modeled by Jesus. It's wise for us to learn and adopt his ways. This isn't a task list to complete, but rather it's a sampling of grace-covered practices to help us become more aware of God's presence and to bring about soul deep transformation.

STUDY

Read the Bible, read a study guide, take classes, listen to a sermon. Observe, interpret, and apply what you learn.

SERVICE

Attend to the needs and concerns of others without the desire for recognition.

CELEBRATION

Delight in God's blessings.

SIMPLICITY

Willingly resist extravagance.

WORSHIP

Reflect and adore the person of God.

MEDITATING

Ponder a verse, phrase, prayer, picture, or word to let it sink in deeply.

Which spiritual discipline would you like to nurture? How might you do that (be specific)?

This is what the Sovereign Lord,
the Holy One of Israel, says:
"Only in returning to me
and resting in me
will you be saved;
In quietness and confidence
is your strength."

ISAIAH 30:15 NLT

GETTING TO KNOW YOU

Learning to walk with Jesus and adopt his rhythms of grace requires showing up and engaging as your fullest, truest self. He created you with a unique combination of personality, preferences, passions, gifts, and talents, and it is good to pay attention to these.

WORDS TO DESCRIBE ME

Personality assessments are helpful tools to help you understand yourself better. What tools have you used? What have you learned?

When completing this list, use this question to help you: If you could never do _____ again, would you miss it? If so, add it to your list!

THINGS I LIKE TO DO

☐   ☐
☐   ☐
☐   ☐
☐   ☐
☐   ☐
☐   ☐
☐   ☐
☐   ☐
☐   ☐
☐   ☐
☐   ☐

Look back over your list and notice themes. Do they include other people, or do they provide opportunities to be alone? Are they creative? Relational? How does this list help you understand yourself better?

In what ways have you been shrinking back, forgetting who you are, and denying your God-given light from shining? Invite the Holy Spirit to show you where you can engage more fully as yourself.

Before my fortieth birthday, it felt important to take the year to participate in little things that I could do just for me. In the midst of normal life, I had grown forgetful of who I was, what I liked, what things brought me joy and what was important to me. I was inspired by a friend to prioritize my own likes, desires, and goals—not to earn accolades, but just to honor the person God made me to be. So I wrote out a list of forty things I wanted to do before I turned forty and called it my 40 x 40 list.

My list was an assortment of inconsequential things like "make sourdough bread" and "whiten my teeth" as well as more heartfelt desires, like "write a children's book" and "heal my gut." I didn't check off every box on my list, yet simply stating the dreams, writing them down and giving them attention felt vital to my growth.

Use this space to write a list of big and little desires. These don't have to be bucket-list items, although they can be! There are no rules for how many items (my uncle did a 6 x 60 list). The whole point is to give yourself space to practice being you, name what you enjoy, and look at yourself with kindness. Simply come up with a list of things that feel important, choose a date you want to complete them by, and then get started checking things off!

MY ___ x ___ LIST

- [ ]
- [ ]
- [ ]
- [ ]
- [ ]
- [ ]
- [ ]
- [ ]
- [ ]
- [ ]
- [ ]
- [ ]
- [ ]
- [ ]
- [ ]
- [ ]
- [ ]
- [ ]
- [ ]
- [ ]

- [ ]
- [ ]
- [ ]
- [ ]
- [ ]
- [ ]
- [ ]
- [ ]
- [ ]
- [ ]
- [ ]
- [ ]
- [ ]
- [ ]
- [ ]
- [ ]
- [ ]
- [ ]
- [ ]
- [ ]

You are a chosen people,
a royal priesthood, a holy nation,
God's special possession,
that you may declare the praises
of him who called you
out of darkness
into his wonderful light.

1 PETER 2:9

Lean in to the mirror.

Do you only see your mistakes or shame?

Your times of loss or wounding?

Keep looking.

The kind and present Jesus will reflect what he sees.

Where you see failure, he sees irreplaceable value.

Where you see imperfection, he sees

forgiveness and generous mercy.

Where you see times of failing others,

he sees a future with peace and love.

Where you see only darkness,

he reveals his glorious light of freedom.

What do you most need to know about God? What do you want to hear from him?

Take a moment to be still before him, close your eyes, take a breath, and describe or draw any pictures or write any words or questions stirring within you today.

WALK IN TRUTH

"My questions of identity and value ran deep. I knew in my head who God said I was, but until I could fully trust and depend on him, I would always dance between belief and doubt."
Freely and Lightly, pages 185–186

How does this idea of dancing between belief and doubt play out in your faith? Your life?

Attributes of God

We get to know God by studying his character. What is he like? Why does he do what he does? Spending time and energy learning more about who God is will build trust that allows you to follow his unforced rhythms of grace.

This is an abbreviated list of the attributes of God. These truths are found in Scripture, and they are on display in creation. *Use the space provided to add Scriptures, details, questions, or experiences that help you know and trust God more.*

God is Creator

God is eternal

God is faithful

God is good

God is gracious

God is holy

God is immutable

God is incomprehensible

God is infinite

God is just

God is love

God is merciful

God is patient

God is perfect

God is Provider

God is righteous

God is sovereign

God is wise

You will keep
in perfect peace
all whose minds
are steadfast
because they trust
in you.

ISAIAH 26:3

How does knowing who God is change the way you see yourself?

WHO YOU ARE IN GRACE

Set aside time to read and savor this. Speak it aloud to remind yourself who you are in Jesus.

The only person whose opinion counts says that I am chosen,[1] known,[2] and loved,[3] and that there is no condemnation for my wandering, forgetful, selfish ways.[4] I am made right with God by placing my faith in Jesus Christ.[5] Nothing can break his love for me,[6] so I know this is true: The righteousness given to me by God results in quietness and confidence forever.[7] This is my new life.[8] No more hustling, striving, or scrambling to measure up and be found worthy.[9] My soul can be quiet because the work is complete.[10] God is faithful, merciful, and gracious,[11] and I can trust with confidence that he is enough,[12] that he is infinitely able,[13] and that he has my best at heart.[14] No matter the circumstances, I am in good hands.[15] He fills me with perfect peace as I trust in him,[16] and because he is the God of hope, I too can overflow with hope by the power of the Holy Spirit.[17] He invites me to come to him, and as I do, he puts my soul at rest.[18] Now to God be all the glory forever and ever, amen.[19]

---

[1] John 15:16
[2] Isaiah 43:1
[3] Zephaniah 3:17
[4] Romans 8:1
[5] Romans 3:22

[6] Romans 8:38-39
[7] Isaiah 30:15
[8] 2 Corinthians 5:17
[9] 1 Peter 2:9
[10] John 19:30

[11] Exodus 34:6
[12] 2 Corinthians 12:9
[13] Ephesians 3:20
[14] Jeremiah 29:11
[15] Philippians 4:12-13

[16] Isaiah 26:3
[17] Romans 15:13
[18] Matthew 11:28-30
[19] Jude 1:25

Of the verses used in the personal offering (see previous page), choose six of these to write out below to further embrace these truths. (Consider writing out the others in another notebook as part of your spiritual disciplines.)

The ability to walk with Jesus, work with him, and learn his rhythms is a direct result of dwelling with, conforming to, remaining in, and abiding with Jesus. *Read John 15 and reflect on what it might look like for you to remain connected to Jesus today.*

God, what a kind and loving God you are. You cover my inadequacies with grace through Jesus, so when you look at me, you see a beautiful reflection. Thank you for calling me out of the dark and into your wonderful light. Lord, remind me when I look to the world, to my efforts, and to my past for my value that you alone are the true source of all joy, peace, and hope. Instead of giving me a checklist to complete, you ask me to be with you. Thank you for your provision of everything I need and for showing me how to walk in step with you.

Amen ♦

PART FOUR

AN INVITATION TO LIVE
FREELY AND LIGHTLY

INTRODUCTION

When our family took an extended road trip around the country, we had a saying: "Heads up!" The kids often watched movies to pass the time on the long drives, but when my husband, Ryan, or I noticed a landmark or sunset, an iconic cityscape or breathtaking view out our car window, we'd call out, "Heads up!" It signaled to the kids to pause the distraction before them and glance upward to experience the beauty they might have otherwise missed.

Sometimes we need this heads-up reminder in our spiritual lives, don't we? Perhaps you could use a friendly nudge or a new habit to help you move your focus away from what's right in front of you and to see from a new perspective. That's what spiritual transformation is all about. It's a rethinking, a refilling, a renewing of the heart, mind, and soul that happens when you lift your eyes off the worries of this world to find God's beauty, goodness, and truth right in the middle of your everyday moments. He is present, and near, and always at work; sometimes it just takes some practice to notice. But when you do, those glimpses of God's glory remind you of who he is, what he says about you, and the purposes he has for you. They build trust, and in turn, set your soul at rest. And that's the end goal, isn't it? To truly live with the quiet confidence of his peace.

It is important to pause and be in awe of God—and to notice the growth that is happening inside you. Like the pencil lines on the doorframe of the pantry where we mark our kids' heights, these little signs may feel insignificant, but as they stack up, we become more and more aware of the growth that is happening. So, my friend, heads up! There is evidence of the work of Jesus within you, and you will find the greatest joy when you celebrate this grace and use your gifts and talents for the good of others and the glory of God.

This is an invitation to live freely and lightly.

Thank you, God, for showing me more of who you are, for delighting in me and giving me a good purpose. May I be a trusting daughter who brings you glory as I walk forward in the knowledge of your love and acceptance. You are offering me a settled peacefulness, a quiet confidence, a contented joy ... and I want to receive those things. Continue to transform my heart to receive your good gifts.

Share your heart with God.

Amen ♥

lightly (adv.):

gently, delicately, or softly

Jesus invites you to live freely and lightly. Share a time when you felt free and light.

Describe a moment when you felt limited, burdened, stuck.

How does it feel to shed light on the contrast between these two feelings and experiences?

What are you most excited about when you think of living freely and lightly?

"When we live in connection to Jesus, we gain a secure, restful, free, and light inner disposition. We practice self-acceptance and are faithful to our path and purpose. We are authentic and obedient. We are present, forgiving, and contented. We show kindness and live generously as our true selves."

Freely and Lightly, page 221

List some of the signs of living freely and lightly. Use the words from the previous page as well as your own.

Where do you see these characteristics showing up in your life?

Right now, which characteristic is your biggest challenge and most important heads-up invitation from the Lord?

I AM LIST

Fill in the blanks with truths about who you are—preferences, desires, qualities, characteristics, and so on. Big and seemingly small things are what make you who you are.

I am

I am

I am

I am

I am

"I am okay, just as I am. You are okay, just as you are. Not because we are wonderful on our own but because God chose us, formed us, dwells in us, delights in us, and calls us his own. We are enough because when he looks at us, he sees a reflection of his own beauty, goodness, and truth." *Freely and Lightly*, page 226

I am

I am

I am

I am

I am

For the Lord your God
is living among you.
He is a mighty Savior.
He will take great delight
in you with gladness.
With his love, he will
calm all your fears.
He will rejoice over you
with joyful songs.

ZEPHANIAH 3:17 NLT

When have you felt God's pleasure in you being you? If you can't recall a moment being immersed in God's delight in who you are just as you are, spend a few moments sensing these words being spoken over you:

" _____ , I am so pleased with who you are. I want you to feel free and light and loved."

Describe any emotions, physical sensations, or thoughts that emerged during this experience.

do your thing

Because God is good and he loves you, he has set within you and equipped you with good, purposeful, meaningful ways to bring him glory and offer beauty, hope, and love to the world.

You desire to use your gifts for the good of others and the glory of God ... but what if you're not sure what your thing is? Use these questions to help you narrow it down.

What do others see in you? What do they ask for your opinion about?

What is something your friends don't like doing but you do? Something you are very good at that others tend to struggle with?

What did you want to be when you grew up? What did you do for fun as a child?

THINGS THAT BRING LIFE

THINGS THAT DRAIN

How can you fill your daily routine with more of what brings you life and less of what doesn't?

GIFT WRAPPING ESSENTIALS

In what ways can you use your life and gifts to benefit others? What is your unique way to share God with the world?

HATS I WEAR

name   _name_

FAVORITE PART   **FAVORITE PART**

LEAST FAVORITE PART   **LEAST FAVORITE PART**

Think of your current roles (the hats you wear). Reflect on what you like, what works and what doesn't.

name

name

FAVORITE PART

FAVORITE PART

LEAST FAVORITE PART

LEAST FAVORITE PART

May the God of hope
fill you with all joy and peace
as you trust in him,
so that you may
overflow with hope
by the power of the Holy Spirit.

ROMANS 15:13

make good choices

Think of all the options, activities, jobs, and responsibilities that lie before you. What are things only you can do? What are things you cannot (or should not!) take on? Invite the Holy Spirit to help you create this list and remind you of who you are, who God is forming you into, and which purposes he has set before you.

MINE TO DO:

NOT MINE:

When making a decision, run it through these questions:

Is this in line with who God says I am?
Am I doing this for affirmation from others?
Does this bring him glory?

Consider a decision you are currently making. Write it here:

_____

_____

In the space below, run it through the three questions above to help you make a decision.

Let everyone be devoted to fulfill the work God has given them to do with excellence, and their joy will be in doing what's right and being themselves, and not in *being affirmed by* others.
Galatians 6:4 TPT

God can use the things about you that you see as weakness, things that you think are not right or are broken, or things that you've been told are not good enough for your good and his glory. All it takes is shifting your identity from what you do and what you say about yourself to who God is and what he says about you.

Can you name something that needs to be redeemed in your heart and mind? What does scripture say about this?

_____

_____

_____

_____

_____

_____

_____

_____

_____

_____

_____

_____

_____

GRATITUDE

Notice the goodness of God in your everyday.

Now to him who is able
to do immeasurably more
than all we ask or imagine,
according to his power
that is at work within us,
to him be the glory in
the church and in
Christ Jesus
throughout all generations,
for ever and ever!
Amen.

EPHESIANS 3:20-21

Signs of Growth

Look for, notice, and name the signs of growth in your life. Celebrate the transformation that is happening inside you!

"Every minute of every day, we get to choose.
Will we forget who we truly are? Will we look to the
world to offer us value, love, and acceptance? Or will we
trust that who God is, who he made us to be, and the purposes he has placed in our hearts are where our true fulfill-
ment rests? Our daily choice to remember, pay attention,
and abide—the tiny acts of faith that collect at the end
of the day, the week, the month, and the year—adds up
to a life of more than just 'fine.' God invites us to a life of
joy, peace, and abundance; it's up to us to accept his gracious invitation. And as we do, his radiant light will work
its wonders and cause us to flourish in the most extraordi-
nary, unimaginable ways."

Freely and Lightly, pages 281–282

Express the truths you commit today to hold, remember, and honor moving forward.

☐

☐

☐

☐

☐

☐

☐

☐

☐

☐

Thank you, Jesus, for the invitation to abundant life. Keep showing me the ways to recover my life, take a real rest, learn the unforced rhythms of grace, and live freely and lightly. When I'm tempted to wander and flirt with distractions that cause me to seek life from other sources, will you remind me, once again, that true satisfaction is found in you? Thank you for being a good and gracious God.

May my life be used for your glory.